MUSINGS IN RHYME

POEMS THAT INSPIRE & STIR YOUR HEART

MOIZ J. QUTBI

Contents

Contents

Acknowledgements

First of all, I would thank our spiritual leader Dr Syedna Aliqadar Mufaddal Saifuddin, whose blessings and prayers are always my source of peace and guidance.

Secondly, my family, for being the constant support and for cheering me at every step.

Mrs Rama Sharma, the teacher who has made me fall in love with the English language. Thank you, for convincing me to continue writing my heart out.

Special mention of Ruqaiya, my partner for life. She has always been an ardent supporter of my writing and continues to inspire me.

Preface

Musings - contemplating, thinking. Our minds are usually filled with thoughts and questions. When we pay heed to these thoughts individually, spending time with them, they turn into musings. What started out as an ordinary challenge of writing a poem a day, slowly turned into opportunities for testing new styles, exploring new themes of writing. For example the poem 'Smoke' gave me the unique challenge of imagining myself as a smoker. The finished poem put doubts in a few near ones about me even picking up the habit. Dear Reader, beyond this page, immerse yourself in the sea of midnight thoughts put in rhyme.

1. Like A Phoenix

He had it all.
Riches, success and everything to make you stand tall.
His life seemed perfect and nothing, he felt, could affect it.
But one day, he was struck by a bolt from fate.
That strikes always at the right time. Never early, nor too late.
And all in a blink, this perfect life is no more what he could think.
When nothing of him remained, except his painful conscience being gagged and chained.
Robbed of every ability,
Lying there silent and quiet.
All he had was his breath.
And the hope to be back someday.
In the silence of the day and the peace of the night.
His hope accompanied with all his might.
In every breath of air,
He whispered a silent prayer.
A prayer to his Maker.
The divine, the Almighty.
Seeking the strength to withstand such a test.
The patience, to bring him out in his best.
With every prayer of thanks,

He found vigour anew.
Discovered the power of faith,
He knew that depending on others may fail
But, the power of a prayer
For only the divine will, in such a way your broken life fix.
To bring you back from the ashes to fly like a Phoenix.

2. The Sunflower

O friend of mine!
Know that the sun doesn't shine all the time.
As with Allah's creations, so is it with our lives.
You may be bright and focused in the bright of light.
But, O friend! The sun sets when,
You must not lose hope then.
Yes, maybe others cannot notice the good in you.
Maybe you look like a dull being without any lustre.
I hope you become like the sunflower.
To wait patiently for the sun to rise.
To seek comfort and warmth from its rays.
Knowing that after the dark of the night,
The sun will always come out to shed on everyone its light.

3. The Dandelion

Excuse me, to my lover,
I want to gift a flower.
To show what I really mean
To tell her that I care.
For her, I'll always be there.
I would not like to go for the rose for it is too common, too clichéd
Do you have something that will tell her,
What my heart hides, without having a word to utter.
I have no riches nor pockets full of dollars.
With a few cents, can I gift her a flower?
Why yes, for just a few cents
You can get the humble dandelion.
I asked, but why do they come so cheap then.
The rose, you see is often sold by the dozen.
While the dandelion is left alone.
Gift this to your love and it will fulfil her wishes.
All she needs to do is, blow at it in the winds.

4. Quest For True Love

I had read of true love.
In fables and tales of yore.
True love, they said never existed.
Something to believe I refused.
Setting out day after day.
With the belief, true love existed somewhere
and in some special way.
The Divine surely put love in His creations.
And just then, my quest brought me to the shores.
With the calm winds that blow
At peace, I find myself, sure and slow.
Cutting out the worldly noise and the clatter,
I hear the waters whisper.
What are you searching for O seeker?
Just as the whisper, my voice I reduced to a murmur.
And said I have been searching for true love.
Can you be my guide so in my quest I can finally find true love?
Where it exists and how.
You are in the right place.
And the answer lies in front of your face.
This got me into deep thinking.
Could it be the clouds up above?

And then it struck and I was sure.
True love as God made it, lies right here on the shore.
The waves, no matter the distance, ride the seas to meet their sandy lover.
Even if it kept them together only for an hour.
Waiting for the right moment and the right winds,
The waves ride towards the shores.
All around the world.
Be it hot or cold,
The loving waves ride with the right winds
To meet their lover.

5. True Bliss

In the search of bliss, many spend their lives,
When it could be lying right in front of their eyes.
Bliss is lying in your mother's lap.
Bliss is the freedom to take an afternoon nap.
Bliss is feeling the wind in your hair.
Bliss is taking a child to the fair.
Bliss is having friends that care.
When life throws its tests at you,
You know, you can get through these times with a smile and your friends by your side.
This is the truest form of bliss.

6. Chasing The Wind

So satisfying feels the wind in your face.
Especially when you are running a race.
These winds are the source of a thrill
That can't be replaced by a drug
Nor replicated by any pill.
The joy of lacing up for a run
Be it for exercise or fun.
All geared up at the starting line,
Man, I'd sure love to be running till I'm 69.
Come young, come old.
Run, to return with stories waiting to be told.
Uphill or downslope,
Choose a route of your liking.
And it doesn't matter if you prefer to go riding.
Life's meant to keep us moving.
A little exercise every day
To keep you happy, healthy out of the grey.
And to stay young within,
My friend, you have to chase the wind.

7. Through These Years

So, I turn a year older.
And I already feel wiser.
Over three decades of life.
Of years filled with joy while also combined with rife.
In every instance, a lesson learned.
While some taught me patience,
Others taught me to build strength.
Never give up and cover the entire length.
Learnt that there are always valuable lessons to gain,
If you can just make it through the pain.
To travel all those miles,
You can accomplish
If you can spread your smiles.
Through these years of life, I've been taught,
To keep smiling even if with troubles, you are fraught.
That little curve on your lips, enough to chase away the sorrows.
Turn your troubles into tiny floating bubbles.
Pop them away with a single tap.
After all these years, I have realized true joy when my children run to sit in my lap.
As I step forward to enter a brand new sphere,
With the one I love, and my heart holds dear.

I am filled with hope and faith anew.
For a future, content and true.

8. A Spark

Sometimes, a spark is all it takes.
To stop a zooming car by hitting the brakes.
Set ablaze a lush garden and reduce it to ashes.
Ruin loving relationships through incessant fights.
Make you lost in reality despite the surrounding lights.
A spark of misunderstanding, a sliver of doubt.
Grows into a fire glaring,
Leaving you love without.
So, my friend, mend your bonds, make them strong.
Let no fire touch you, seem however small.
Let the strong bonds keep you standing firm and tall.

9. Strength Of A Mountain

When the skies are cloudy,
Winds are blowing terribly,
It's pouring like there's no end.
Don't you falter, my friend.
Strong and tall like a mountain, you must stand.
When falling seems the easier option,
Choose instead, the courage of the mountain.
Rain, snow, whatever be the weather,
To shake this bold structure, nothing will be able ever.
Instilled with deep faith and roots firm in the ground.
When you are going through a storm,
My friend, let not your faith be battered and torn.
All your trust in the One above, place you must.
Unclear they may seem now,
His plans for you shall make you shine like a star.
The highest ranks you will attain.
If in tough times you show the strength of a mountain.

10. Smoke

Oh, the rush of everyday work!
The hustle seems endless with no rest
Everyone is in a race to the top to be the best.
I stare at the clock with empty eyes tick tock.
Why do the minutes take ages?
Finally, it is time o clock.
My palms sweaty I get the roll out with a struggle.
My lips touch the roll and I look back at the hustle.
The smoke seems to liberate me.
Going into my lungs and coming out leaving me free.
How I love floating in the air like the smoke from my lips.
Many times I have been told to give this habit a quit?
How do I tell them that the smoke frees me as it leaves my lungs?
Such short-lived pleasures are those of smoke.

11. Start Over Again

My friend, life may not always be clear skies and sunshine.
It may throw surprises at you when you feel all is going fine.
These challenges, you must dodge if forward you want to move.
Your grit and strength, all tested if yourself as a champion you want to prove.
Don't you falter, don't you bend. Look to God and in Him, you'll find a friend.
T help you up, to make amends.
But, all this, only when you have the courage to do it all over again.
Like a clean sheet, you have your new life with you.
The Champion that has successfully every obstacle been through.
Bouncing back from a failure is possible and it has been proven,
If only my friend, you do not hesitate to start over again.

12. Alone

We avoid company often.
Feel like we are better off alone.
Yes, the peace from the chatter,
The noise and the clatter
Is sometimes a much-needed break.
And to fall in love with your own company,
No better thing could be any.
That's when being lonely becomes a thing of the past.
You are the source of your own happiness and comfort.
As our elders always say,
Loving yourself is finding the perfect love from others in the best way.
My friends, in this world full of troubles and difficulties,
We all need that someone to rely on, right when we need them the most.
It's not easy to make it alone.

13. To Be A Poet

The art of weaving words,

that takes the readers through different worlds

Possessed by a few, though the art isn't new.

But what does it mean to be a poet?

Let me put it on paper so you too know it.

A poet feels way more than a normal man.

He even tries to imagine feelings whenever he can.

With every poem, he pens down,

A piece of his soul in ink he drowns.

Reliving moments from his life through the written words.

Memories that may be as sweet as birds,

Or unpleasant, painful and bitter.

Events that make him cringe and shudder.

But, he must to his pen bestow them,

To share this art with the avid reader.

For only after reading can you discover a hidden gem.

Poets with their play of words can help you fly.

Put a smile on your beautiful face even when you want to cry.

The beauty of well-spun words lies in the heart of the poet.

That he pours out in his poems so the readers too can know it.

14. To Bloom

Do you feel you have not reached your potential?
Looking at the other roses,
While you've yet to gain a petal.
And every time you are deprived of greatness.
Of titles and honours.
My friend, Allah has set for all great plans.
You may be on the right path.
Stick to it for success.
We are like a bud hanging from a mighty plant.
Be patient and pray that He, your wishes grants.
You shall see greatness soon.
And none can take what's yours when it is your time to bloom.

15. A Prayer

Oh Divine! I come tonight with a prayer.
A silent wish, my heart's desire.
Through storms I have been.
Many dark days I have seen.
Tonight, Oh creator, I thank you.
Thank you for the life you've gifted.
Thank you for the times I was down and yet, because of You, I was lifted.
Allah! I stand here with a humble heart and a silent prayer.
Please oh please give me an answer. Tell me You're there.
I keep telling myself these tests
are only to bring out my inner best.
Please reassure me that this is right.
Show me the path through this dark night.
People say that man remembers God only when times are tough.
Everyday prayed to You, I have.
Sitting through the storms, firm and quiet.
One thing that kept me going was my faith.
And now, with my grit and will tested,
Time and again, I was to the right path redirected.
My heart brims with gratitude.
I thank you.

Thank you for the hurdles that have made me stronger.
Even though the path is tough and to reach, I might take longer.
I know one thing. That You will get me there.

16. I Know An Angel

She tasted of mornings, I would tell her always.
Of slithering dew drops on leaves.
Ah her smell! She smelled of freshly watered lavender.
Her voice, so soft and tender
Like the call of a cuckoo perched high on a branch.
Her eyes had in them such depth,
Like a vault with treasures safely kept.
She glides across the room and gives me a promising glance, as I approach her for a dance
She is a girl that dreams are made of.
Soft and gentle on the inside and if needed, can be tough.
There is one thing I could surely tell.
She is nothing short of an angel.
She took away my heart and I was under her spell.

17. Dreamy Girl

There hails a girl
From the city of pearls.
To the art of daydreaming, she is no stranger.
And if you've known her longer
Drifting away to her fairyland can you see.
She could be in her room,
Arranging her books on the shelves,
And poof, she has turned into snow White, surrounded by the elves.
When at school, in the midst of her classes,
A simple object like the ceiling fan
could whirl her away on adventures with Peter Pan.
Even though this dame may seem,
To always be engrossed in her daydream,
She is one with a vision.
And through her bouts of daydreams, finds motivation.
To go after her goals with rigour anew.
Tick off the challenges she has been through.
Only to come out as one of the stars.
Shining brighter and also help as a guiding light to others.

18. Wings For Life

Once there was a time.
Shackled in chains was I.
Any movement was a big struggle.
Felt like I was trapped in a bubble.
Robbed off the gift of speech.
Normalcy seemed completely out of reach.
Days and weeks passed by
While the struggles heard only a silent cry.
But, the Blessed one arrived with help.
Like an angel floating through the air.
Gave voice that turned into a roar from a welp.
Snipped off the chain.
To be replaced with wings.
And I felt free again.
Running with the wind.
Oh where could these wings take me?
To faraway lands or a strange country?
High above the clouds,
No ounce of doubt my mind shrouds.
Patience & faith in the One up there,
can give you wings.
Go fly faraway to a land free of care and full of beautiful things.

19. Flower Power

There's darkness all around,
Nothing you can hear, not a single sound.
The walls are closing in,
Pressure's too much to bear.
Put your faith in the One above
His plans are in the working all year.
Like water for a seed beneath the ground.
It is faith that you need, to keep yourself safe and sound.
First, there comes a shoot and you make your way towards the light.
Stick to the struggle, however hard seems it might.
Every day you grow stronger and the world is yours to conquer.
Spread the fragrance of your blooming flower,
Proof that you are not one to hide.
The testimony of your power, wear this badge with pride.

20. Twinkle In Her Eyes

Seen a lot of pretty faces,
Ain't nothing like her,
To the girl with a twinkle in her eyes and knotted silky hair.
Our chats fathomed even the abyss' depth.
Of dreams and wishes in a vault safely kept.
To be opened sometime in future.
Maybe when we are together.
She stole my love, she stole my heart.
With promises of never being apart.
And though now we may be miles away,
Our faith lies strong that the future
will see us together in a bond that with time grows stronger.
And it all started with the Twinkle in her eyes.

21. Lucky I Found You

Meeting you is the best that has happened to me.
Oh, how I longed to be in your company.
Your voice lifts me up when I'm down.
My love, with you, my face never wears a frown.
It is only you that helps me see a future,
With the arrival of joy.
and sorrow's departure.
May Allah bless those eyes,
Even in my faults, only virtue you see.
You give me the strength and confidence to take on any challenge we may meet.
As long as you are beside me,
I can hold my head high while firm on the ground remain my feet.
My love, my life partner,
You make me happy like no other.

22. Love Heist

Most people swear by love at first sight,
Love, it makes your days bright.
We started with awkward hellos.
Soon we were into talks late at night.
The moon, the stars, they all seemed to be positioned right,
for she slowly became my symphony.
Her sweet songs engulfed me right from the start.
No longer in its place I could feel my heart,
Cupid had struck and played his part.
For I was hers and she mine.
As I witnessed the greatest love heist of all time.

23. My World Has Changed

When I felt free as a bird,
I felt alone, none listened to my word.
And I wondered they would certainly be different if I moulded myself for them.
Only half aware of losing myself in the process.
Fate played its game and I was no longer the same.
This bird was now robbed and had been caged.
Oh how my World changed!

This new and different self
Felt so odd and strange.
To mingle with others, he felt obliged.
Every day a different life,
learning to cope with the effects of strife.
Settling down to the new normal,
How my world has changed

Then, I happened to come across an angel.
She glided into my life and cast on me her loving spell.
Day after day with this pretty dame

Filled me with hope and removed my fears.
Even though I met her just now,
It felt like I'd known her for years.
Now, calls her, every beat of my heart.
Longing to see her dressed in Vermillion as my bride.
Live a magical life with this angel by my side.
And I know, she has changed my world.

24. Ode To My Comfort Food

Oh, my jalebi!
You sweet, twisted, orange beauty.
Whenever I am down, you lift me up.
How you manage to do it every time beats me.
Holding your coiled body with my fingers gets the taste buds geared.
Your dripping sweetness that could give honey a run for its money.
Every time you unpack yourself at my table and a whiff of yours I get,
Your sugary fragrance makes my worries whoosh like a jet.
You lift me up and help make amends,
Like a phone call from a close friend.
Oh, my dear jalebi! Your intriguing shape and sweetness put a smile on my lips no matter what my mood.
This is why you are undisputedly my favourite comfort food.

25. Lessons From Failure

They say victory tastes sweet.
Like an old friend, it comes over to meet.
Yes, we all love the thrill of winning.
To be held high and our mouth, always grinning.
But, my friend, the joy of coming out victorious
after rock bottom failure is tremendous.
Winning, without failure brings in pride.
Makes one haughty and privileged in his stride.
Where there exist only good times,
people do not value things, nor do they dare to tread out of the lines.
On the other hand, failure teaches you.
It sifts out the fake friends from the ones that are true.
Failure teaches you to be humble.
To be strong when the world around you crumbles.
Every failure, shows you your mistake.
How you can correct it and again you do not repeat.
Through these lessons you come out stronger and better.
To agree undoubtedly that Victory after a failure is the sweetest treat.

26. When Our Time Comes

Someday when my lights go down,
And this world ceases to exist around.
Flashes and flashes before my eyes.
Of all those years and the rush of memories.
Oh what will I see before my eyes shut never to open.
Will I smile from the happy days I've seen?
Or will my brow frown from the storms through I've been?
Many lessons have I learnt in life the hard way.
At times I questioned if I'd see the next day.
But, life teaches things so important and true.
To focus on the good and the ones close to you.
There will be times, both good and bad,
Memories to be made forgetting those that made us sad.
Forever grateful for my loved ones will I be,
Through thick and thin they're always with me.
So, when it's time to leave,
I'll go happy and thankful for the time I'd had to live.
Let there be no tears
Know that I've given my best all these years.
They say life is a game played by our fate.

Smile, live happy before it's too late.

27. Class Clown

He was, to all, known
As the class clown.
For no day passed ever,
without him being the cause of thunderous laughter.
Loved by teachers and mates alike.
He was the reason even boring lectures seemed bright.
His jokes and comments were well thought and executed right.
Making sure none were hurt or feelings played with.
But, this clown had a dark story behind his infectious smile.
He may hide his pain, but his eyes spoke truth all the while.
Going through unbearable pain at times.
He sought refuge in spreading smiles.
If only, somebody bothered to look at his eyes.
To know his story and how his smile is a cover of lies.
If only, someone cared to recognise the pain hiding behind his laughter.
This clown could have lived a life better.
But, till the time someone hugs him hard enough to set his broken pieces right.
He will dawn the role of the clown and spread smiles come what might...

28. Ode To My Chin

It's been so long since I last saw you.
Over a decade since we bid adieu.
When I was just half my age.
Only a few years into my teenage.
So many new things in life and so much change.
For this face was now wearing a mane.
No more was I just a kid.
This beard gave me the title of a man.
An everyday sight you were in the mirror, no more could you be seen.
Neighbour to my smile, my chin.
Slowly but surely covered by the thick foliage.
Bringing in the looks of a sage.
I remember holding you high up in the air.
As a symbol of pride.
Now you lie hidden deep under thick, tangled hair.
Slowly and surely as the mane grows, makes me wonder
What it was like having a beardless face.
Now, I have accepted its warm embrace.
Covering, protecting half my face.
My beard glorifies my identity
And it is here to stay.

29. My Journey In Verse

It started with a thought. Any longer I could keep within me not.
So, I put my faith in the humble pen.
O give me a source to outpour my pain.
Line after line, my feelings in ink fell into rhyme to be called a poem.
Poem after poem the more I wrote, the more I felt my heart at ease.
There were also times when rhymes would in my dreams, come to tease.
Why don't you write this? You should have done that.
And mornings would see a brand new poem in my head.
Waiting to be inked, longing to be read.
Soon my writing had gained a following and readers waiting for a new release.
Gaining momentum all over the nation.
I found a larger audience for my work soon.
Recognition and accolades came like a magnet.
For soon, from a beginner, I turned into a published poet
O Allah I thank thee for your gifts of fame and respect.
I pray that the power of the pen shall with me be forever,
That I keep writing to inspire beautiful minds all over.

30. The Gift Of An Artist

It is indeed a gift,
to transform the world as an artist.
When you can feel the music in the winds.
When you find beauty even in tiny things.
How you conjure a masterpiece out of thin air?
How do you feel things that weren't there?
Notice the tiniest of differences in what's around.
How do you keep your chin in the air while your feet are firmly on ground?
All your goodies safely tucked under your belt of humility.
This world is your canvas, plain and white.
How do you bring in the perfect blend of colours in the right amount of strokes?
No one can make out an artist's masterpiece in the midst of his works.
It is only after he finishes the whooshing and the slashing of his trusted tool.
How do you pick the right strings to create a soulful symphony?
When the world is in chaos and everywhere is cacophony.
Oh, artist your skilful strumming,
has got everyone humming to your tunes
even along their daily routine.

And that paper which was all dull and white,
Your colours have created on it a multi-chromatic delight.
Indeed it is a gift to be an artist.

31. My Parallel Universe

Somewhere in a different dimension,
Exists a parallel universe.
Much similar to ours,
but, after a closer look,
One will notice many things that make it a place totally different.
For one, the deer is the hunter
And the lion, the hunted.
Traffic stops at Green,
and moves at red.
Girls wear shirts,
and the boys are seen in skirts.
No birds in the skies as they would be swimming in the seas.
Replaced by giant whales that fly.
And if I were to explore the possibility
Of a parallel universe for me.
This peaceful Mo'iz would be seen rioting on the road,
While brandishing his sword.
In his life, there'd be no place for a pen,
Totally uninterested in writing would he be then.
His favourite snack, the two minute Maggi,
replaced with cookies made from ragi.

From aiming to run a marathon,
he'd instead be on his couch, binge eating salted popcorn.
And yes, they have rightly said.
The parallel universe is a scary place to tread.

9 798886 410792

Printed by Libri Plureos GmbH in Hamburg, Germany